BACKWARD$ BOOK LAUNCH

Reverse Engineer Your Book and Unlock It's Hidden 6-FIGURE POTENTIAL

MICHELLE KULP

ISBN: 978-1082479632

Table of Contents

FREE GIFT FOR MY READERS

I have a special gift for my readers! If you would like a copy of the *templates and checklists* I created for writing a book a month so you can generate 6-figure royalties, join my private Facebook group. The FREE gift includes:

- **Annual Publishing Chart** to plan your books for an entire year.
- **Income Tracking Chart** to record your income for an entire year.
- **Book Creation Template** to outline each of your books.
- **16 Rapid Writing Secrets** to help you write your books done fast.
- **Bestseller Checklist** to follow so all your books will become Amazon Bestsellers.

JOIN THE GROUP NOW
Facebook.com/groups/28BooksTo100K/

Dedication

This book is dedicated to all of my amazing clients and bestselling authors! They are passionate, creative, brilliant, and fun to work with! I'm so happy to be part of their book-creation journey.

Introduction

There is hidden money tucked away inside your book — to the tune of six, seven, and even eight figures! The good news is that you hold the key to unlocking this money!

Whether you have already published a book or you're considering publishing a book in the future, know that all authors face the same problem…

How to Actually Make Money With Their Books!

Unfortunately, most authors have what I call "One-Dimensional" thinking about making money with their books. They naively believe ALL the money comes solely from book royalties.

This limited thinking keeps the majority of authors broke.

The reality is times have changed, and we've come a long way since the days of traditional publishing, where the gatekeepers (large publishing houses and literary agents) had all the power. With the advent of self-publishing resources like Amazon Kindle Direct Publishing (KDP) and IngramSpark, everything has changed.

Now YOU have ALL the POWER.

The question is: Are you going to use it?

Like the music industry, the publishing industry has changed radically. Musicians no longer only make money from albums or song sales. Now they profit in a multitude of ways such as:

- **Live shows/tours**
- **Physical merchandise**
- **Digital merchandise**
- **Performance royalties**
- **Licensing**
- **YouTube**
- **Sponsorships**
- **Session work**
- **Crowdfunding**
- **Streaming pay-outs**
- **And more!**

It's time for authors to start seeing their books as a more prominent gateway to multiple streams of income.

Apple® Technology

Think about Apple. They don't sell *one* product; they have a *SUITE* of products, such as iPads, iPods, iPhones, iMacs, MacBooks, and more!

Apple has what's known as an ***Integrated Product Suite.***

Apple offers a myriad of products, and once a customer purchases their first Apple product and becomes a fan, they typically buy more of the company's products.

I know this because my kids convinced me to leave my flip phone behind and invest in an iPhone several years ago.

I initially fought buying an iPhone because I didn't know much about it, and I thought I wouldn't like it. Quite frankly, I didn't want to expend the energy to learn something new. However, my persuasive kids convinced me to make the change. Now, I own an iPad, a mini iPad, a MacBook, a 27" iMac, and an iPhone.

In this book, I want to teach you how to create an *Integrated Product Suite* around your book, similar to what Apple has. By doing this, you can literally transform your book into a 6-figure and beyond business!

My goal is to help you multiply your book's income 10x by Reverse Engineering the PROFIT into your book first, thereby *creating multiple income streams.*

A book can be a magnetic tool that attracts new readers, followers, leads, and clients directly to your business. After reading this book, you will know exactly how to set it up for your business.

I've been running my Amazon Bestseller program, **BestSellingAuthorProgram.com**, since January 2013 and have done over 300 book launches and helped my clients become

#1 bestselling authors! I have also helped clients become Wall Street Journal and USA Today bestselling authors. I love helping my clients transform their books into money-making machines.

One of my clients, Matthew David Hurtado (who is a case study in this book), tripled his product sales in his Vitamin and Supplement Company due to his #1 bestselling book and went from being a 6-figure author-preneur to a 7-figure author-prenuer!

Matthew also launched a coaching program when he published his #1 bestselling book. To date, that program has sold out.

I promise you can do the same if you follow the steps I outlined in this book.

Don't miss out on opportunities because you want to do things the old way or fear the unknown.

Be an action taker and do it immediately. You have the power to build a 6-figure and beyond business with your book if you do it correctly.

Let's take a look at the old way of doing book launches vs. the new method.

The **OLD paradigm** of a *traditional book launch* **is:**

Publish, Promote, and then maybe make a **Profit** from royalties. The average author earns less than $500 per month in royalties from their book unless, of course, they are a celebrity or a Super-Marketer.

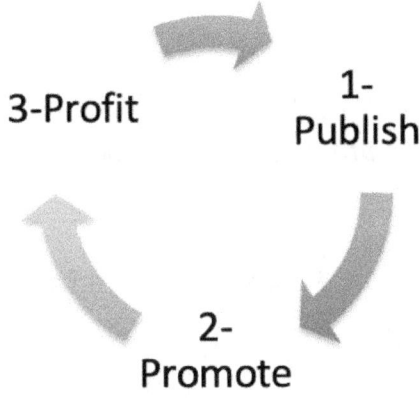

3-Profit   **1-Publish**

2-Promote

The New paradigm for Book Launches is:

Design your **Profit Path** first, then **Publish,** then **Promote.**

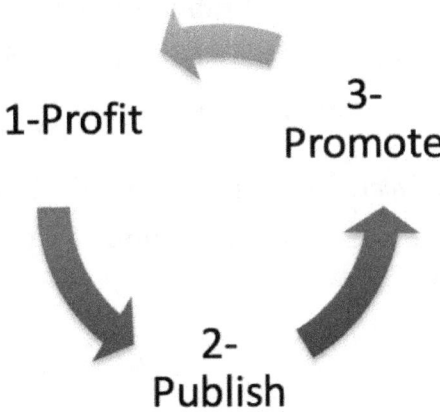

1-Profit   **3-Promote**

2-Publish

NOTE: You can implement profit paths into a previously published book.

3 Steps to the Backwards Book Launch method:

Step 1: Design the Profit Path for your book.

Step 2: Publish your book the right way.

Step 3: Promote your book and become a #1 Bestselling Author.

To make six figures plus with your book, it's paramount to *reverse-engineer the profit into your book at the beginning rather than at the end.*

For most authors, the book's *profit* is an afterthought instead of the first thought.

We are living in an Uber- and Amazon-dominated world. To realize your dreams and goals, you must embrace this new world and leave behind the old world and your *old thinking*.

Instead of *hoping* you will make money solely from book royalties, I will teach you how to build profit paths organically and creatively into your book.

Using my *Backwards Book Launch* method, you will create something valuable and critical to your **long-term success** as an author.

BUSINESS ASSETS

Imagine being a 6-figure author and being able to reach and impact hundreds and perhaps thousands of people with your book's message.

How good will that feel?

Being a broke author serves no one. In fact, it keeps you invisible and keeps your message hidden from the people who need it most.

It's time to change that now.

Smart entrepreneurs, including coaches, consultants, software developers, doctors, healers, accountants, lawyers, high-level business owners, and speakers, are using my *Backwards Book Launch* method to cash in on their knowledge and expertise to the tune of an additional six figures plus from their book.

This book contains four detailed case studies of Smart Entrepreneurs who have built their 6 to 8-figure empires on the backend of their books.

I think the consensus among most entrepreneurs these days is that writing and publishing a book is one of the best ways to become an *"author-ity"* in their field and elevate their ibility. However, it doesn't have to end there.

Remember this…

People are Inundated with INFORMATION
but are Hungry for TRANSFORMATION.

Reading a book filled with great content and information can be transformational, but only if the readers actually apply and implement what they learn.

For many readers, it stops there.

They read a book and love the content, but often need the author's (expert's) help to implement the strategies outlined in the book to get them to the next level.

Authors everywhere are missing a huge opportunity to help their readers on a deeper level with the book's message. They are doing their readers (and potential customers) a dis-service if they don't have a follow-up program built on the back end of their book.

Here's an example…

Years ago, I purchased author Perry Marshall's 268-page book, *The Ultimate Guide to Facebook Advertising: How to Access 1 Billion Potential Customers in 10 Minutes*. I was completely overwhelmed and confused by the information, so I took no action with the information contained in the book.

If the author had offered an online course, a coaching pro-gram, or done-for-you services where I could receive help implementing the information from his book, I would have gladly invested more money with him.

At the time, Perry Marshall did *not* have a program on the backend of his book.

I recently did some research and discovered that Perry Marshall now offers *"Facebook University"*, a membership program for $59 per month. Now he has a direct profit path from his book to his membership program! (He actually has many offerings related to his books which give him multiple streams of income.)

Perry Marshall says that publishing his first book was the best decision he ever made in his business and that it took him from being a *nobody* to a *somebody* – a highly paid expert in his field. He said that having a book allowed him to increase his consulting fees by over 500% and create multiple income streams from his programs.

I'm so excited to teach you how to go from being a broke author to a rich author so you can 10x your income, impact, and influence!

Here's a sampling of what you'll discover in this book:

- How a guy who wrote a book about Pumpkin Patches is now making 7-figures on the backend of his books.

- How an entrepreneur went from flat broke to an 8-Figure Business by giving away FREE books.

- How a computer nerd used his books to attract thousands of followers and built a 7-figure business with multiple streams of income.

- How a guy suffering from complications of Lyme Disease used a #1 bestselling book to revitalize his product business to the tune of 7 figures and build a brand-new coaching platform to the tune of 6 figures.

- 12 Profit Paths you can add to your book right now to generate an additional 6 to 7 figures in revenue.

- **Bonus: 100 Ways to Make $100k**

- How investing eight hours per year can add six figures in revenue from your book.

- How NOT to write income-blocking books (which most authors do).

- The three types of income-producing books you should be writing.

- How a $37 per month program is generating $166,000 per month for one Author-Preneur.

- How to add on as many profit paths to your book as you want so you can 10x your income.

- Why shorter books are better and how you can realistically write a book a month.

- The three steps to implement the Backwards Book Launch.

Let's get started…

Chapter 1

Four Case Studies of 6-Figure+ Author-Preneurs

There's no need to reinvent the wheel when it comes to making HUGE profits from your book.

In this chapter, I will introduce you to four brilliant author-preneurs who not only have written amazing books but have built six-figure empires and beyond around their bestselling books, and one of them is a client of mine!

First up is…

Profit First by Mike Michalowicz

Mike Michalowicz is a genius. Seriously, I love this guy!

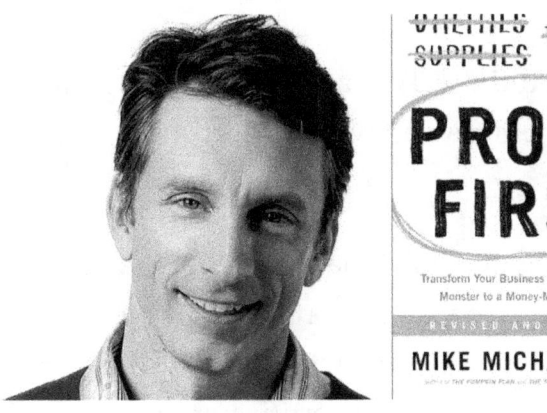

I picked up his book *Profit First: Transform Your Business from a Cash-Eating Monster to a Money-Making Machine* at Barnes and Noble one day. Then, about a week later, I picked up another one of his books, *The Pumpkin Plan: Simple Strategies to Grow a Remarkable Business in Any Field*.

I read **Profit First** in about a week and was very impressed.

In **Profit First**, Mike teaches readers (business owners) why the traditional accounting method of **Sales – Expenses = Profit** is not just contrary to human behavior but is a myth that locks people into a never-ending cycle of *selling more yet profiting less.*

Profit First actually flips the formula (very similar to what I'm doing here with the **Backwards Book Launch** – flipping the traditional formula) and shows business owners the new way to have a profitable business: **Sales – Profit = Expenses**.

Of course, Mike provides multiple case studies throughout his book detailing readers who have applied the *Profit First Formula*, transforming, and in some cases saving their failing businesses.

I love that he didn't STOP at just writing a great book. He knew that business owners would need help implementing his teachings.

Instead of being the only one who could teach his methods to others through coaching, consulting, or even an online course, Mike created a **High-Ticket Certification Program** on the backend of his book. He certifies accountants, financial planners, business coaches, and other professionals who meet his criteria to teach his *Profit First Formula.*

There is no pricing on his website for the cost of the certification program, but my estimate is it's about $10K. At the time of this writing, Mike has certified 128 people. Estimating $10K per person for certification would be an additional profit of over $1 million!

In addition, he offers an affiliate program so that others can sell his services for a portion of the sales, allowing him to make money from other people's efforts.

I don't know the details of his certification program as there are many ways to structure these types of offerings, but he may also be taking a revenue share and/or a yearly renewal fee for his program.

It's a brilliant strategy to add six or seven figures to your book's profit.

Certifications Are a Huge Income Generator for *Profit First*

Here's what Mike says about his certification program in his book:

"As of this very second, there are 128 accountants, bookkeepers, and coaches working hand in hand with me to guide entrepreneurs on an implementation of Profit First. (No worries. You can absolutely do this on your own, but for some people, having an account-

ability partner who knows the ins and outs of their industry who can guide them step-by-step is a better approach.) Of these 128 Profit First Professionals (PFPs), on average we have directed the Profit First implementation of ten companies per PFP. That means we have guided 1,280 businesses to success using Profit First."

I'm sure you're starting to see the BIG picture here.

By certifying others in his teachings, Mike is able to reach and impact the masses.

Brilliant, right?

I'm considering hiring a PFP (Profit First Professional) for my business because I really believe in Mike's teachings and philosophy (and I hate all things related to accounting.)

Throughout Mike's book, he is constantly adding value and building his email list by offering resources by visiting his website.

Mike's other BIG profit path with his book is speaking engagements. Here is what Mike says:

"Helping you and all of our fellow entrepreneurs become more profitable is my life's purpose. I am flying all over America and beyond to speak about Profit First. Tomorrow I will speak to more than 1,100 pharmacy owners at an event in Houston, then to 25 people (if I am lucky) in Casper, Wyoming, then over to New Orleans to talk with 200 folks in the morning and then a panic dash (via plane, train and Uber) to Washington, D.C, for an evening keynote. Then I'll

travel abroad for a few more events. In between, I will do interviews for about four podcasts a day, recording my own podcast (ahem— The Profit First Podcast, of course) and updating this book at night. I do all of these with joy. I will teach this to anyone and everyone."

Mike has not only built a 7-figure empire around his book, *Profit First,* and his teachings. He has truly created a movement.

> **Think about what MOVEMENT you can create with your book.**

Mike Michaelowicz is transforming lives, and I'm proud of him for that.

The truth of the matter is…

> *The book is not the end; the book is just the beginning.*

From what I see, Mike has at least four streams of income (in addition to royalties) from *Profit First*:

1. **Certification Program**

2. **Speaking Engagements**

3. **Possible Revenue share with his Certification program and/or licensing or annual fees**

4. **Affiliate Program**

He has created similar profit paths with his book *The Pumpkin Plan*.

Those interested can become a *Certified Pumpkin Plan Strategist* by application and invitation only.

Mike markets his certification program to coaches, entrepreneurs, teachers, trainers, speakers, and anyone who wants to start, build, or grow their business with a methodology to teach (his).

It's a brilliant approach to building a 7-figure business with a book!

I'm sure ideas of how you can add huge streams of income to your book(s) are spinning in your mind right now.

Our next case study involves a Peak Performance Coach you may have heard of…

Brendon Burchard has the ultimate rags-to-riches story.

Brendon Burchard, Peak Performance Coach

Brief introduction to Brendon:

"After suffering depression and surviving a car accident at the age of 19, Brendon faced what he felt were life's last questions: 'Did I live fully? Did I love openly? Did I make a difference?' His intention to be happy with the answers led to his personal breakthroughs, and ultimately to his life's purpose of helping others live, love and matter. He spent his 20s researching psychology and leadership, and consulting at Accenture. By age 32, he had struck out on his own and become a #1 best-selling author, an in-demand high performance coach, a sought-after speaker, and an early pioneer in the online education space.

"Widely considered one of the most successful early pioneers in online education, Brendon runs an 8-figure multi-media training company. He launched million-dollar online courses in 2009, and he has now passed 17 consecutive online promotions that generated more than 7 figures of revenue in less than seven days each. He shares his knowledge publicly and also privately advises many of the best online marketers in the world via Experts Academy."

Highlights about Brendon:

- Brendon Burchard is one of the top motivation and marketing trainers in the world. –Larry King

- Top 25 Most Influential Leaders in Personal Growth and Achievement. –*Success Magazine*

- Top 100 Most Followed Public Figure in the World. –Facebook Insights

- One of the most influential leaders in the field of personal growth. –O, *The Oprah Magazine*

- The world's leading high-performance coach. –Oprah.com

Brendon has a very powerful story.

What has brought Brendon to that high-level expert status are his bestselling books and how brilliantly he leverages them by attracting raving fans and generating a massive email list by giving away his books for FREE!

He ultimately gives away almost every book he writes for FREE to build up his massive email list and sell products on the backend of those books.

When Brendon's book was rejected by a major Publisher...

*"Brendon famously fought for his art when a major publisher turned down his last book, **The Motivation Manifesto**. This book has since spent over 30 weeks on The New York Times Bestseller List after debuting #1 on BN.com. It's now the bestselling motivation title of this century."*

Brendon's other New York Times bestselling books include:

- *The Charge: Activating the 10 Human Drives that Make You Feel Alive*

- *The Millionaire Messenger*

- *Life's Golden Ticket*

His books have been #1 on every major bestseller list, including Amazon.com, BN.com, USA Today, and The Wall Street Journal.

Over 1,500,000 people have downloaded his books, white papers, and eBooks, and his work has been translated into 25+ languages. His latest book is **High Performance Habits: How Extraordinary People Become That Way."**

And guess what? He's giving it away for FREE!

Brendon's 7-Figure Sales Funnel

A few years ago, I decided to reverse engineer Brendon's sales funnel to determine exactly how he was making seven figures from his book, **The Charge: Activating the 10 Human Drives that Make You Feel Alive.**

Here's what I discovered:

- Brendon did massive free and paid promotions to drive people to a landing page for the FREE copy of his physical book, *The Charge.*

- After signing up and providing all your information (name, email, address, phone number, etc.), he would ship the book to you for the cost of *shipping and handling only.*

- In addition to the book, buyers would receive the following FREE Bonuses:

- o Three videos on how Millionaires succeed

- o The 1-Page Productivity guide (the secret weapon used by CEOs worldwide to regain control of their days and reach their goals faster).

- o A "One Time" offer page with a 90% discount on his High-Performance Training Course that he normally sells for $997. You can get it for $99. If you don't get it right then, you will never see this offer again.

- Following that offer, buyers are put into his autoresponder series, consisting of the following:

#1 – Training Video #1 Delivered with a *Thank You* message

#2 – Training Video #2 Delivered

#3 – Training Video #3 Delivered

#4 – Invite to Sign Up for Brendon's Master's Course that requires you to watch a long video before being directed to the sales page; the cost of that course is $997.

#5 – Another video explaining why you should sign up for his $997 Master's Course

#6 - Final Video about the Master's Course

The above outlines the 7-Figure Sales Funnel Brendon uses to make money on the backend of his book.

He launches the book to #1 by pre-selling the book and having a landing page with extra bonuses for pre-orders. Once he has achieved *bestselling author* status, he gives the book away for FREE to build a massive email list.

Also, when I received Brendon's book, the package included some additional sales materials to promote his programs.

Two million students have completed Brendon's online courses and video series. He is impacting the masses.

I love the strategy of a one-time low offer because, for many, anything under $100 is a no-brainer. He likely makes six figures on that offer alone.

Those in his high-ticket $997 Master's program probably have access to join higher level and higher-cost programs.

Many entrepreneurs at this level can command fees for their private coaching and/or mastermind groups in excess of six figures!

What can you create as a one-time offer to sell on the backend of your book?

Many times, you can re-purpose videos, audios, and training materials from other programs you have.

Brendon sold a recording of a presentation that he had previously given to others who paid $997 for it, creating a high perceived value.

This formula of giving away his print book must be a big moneymaker because he does it for just about every book he publishes.

I recently saw Brendon promoting his book on habits and was giving away several bonuses to those who purchased his book during the pre-order period.

Once the book becomes a #1 bestseller, he will most likely start giving away that book.

Giving away a book that is a *bestseller* is a great way to build your email list fast. *Who doesn't want a FREE book from a bestselling author, right?*

You can also use Facebook ads to drive traffic to a landing page where you give away your book.

It's important to become a #1 bestselling author because once your book hits the Amazon bestsellers list, it's on Amazon's radar. Your book goes from being invisible to visible. Amazon's internal marketing kicks in, and they start promoting your book in a myriad of ways.

Amazon uses an internal algorithm which I believe has to do with reviews, sales, downloads, keywords, and categories.

It's a very powerful system that you can't buy your way into. Amazon rewards bestselling authors by promoting their books to members and customers.

Our next case study is an Internet Marketing Entrepreneur who sells software on the backend of his books. Again, you may have heard of him…

Russell Brunson, The Sales Funnel Guy

Russell Brunson didn't start by writing and publishing books, but he quickly watched other 7-figure Author-Preneurs profit from giving away FREE books, so he followed in their footsteps.

Multiple books with Multiple Streams of Income

To date, Russell Brunson, creator of **ClickFunnels,** has written the following books and sold over 1,000,000 copies:

- *Expert Secrets*
- *DotCom Secrets*
- *108 Proven Split Test Winners*

- *Funnel Stacking: The 3 Core Funnels and How They Work Together*

I've been running an online business since 2005, and I know the biggest concept entrepreneurs struggle to grasp and learn is sales funnels.

Russell Brunson is a master in sales funnels. He makes a fortune teaching everything he knows about sales funnels, such as certifying coaches in sales funnel training, advanced funnel training programs, and more.

His big money maker is his ClickFunnels® software that currently sells for $97 or $297 per month, depending on what features you want.

I love that Russell is writing books to drive sales for his software.

It reminds me of Robert Kiyosaki, author of *Rich Dad, Poor Dad,* who years ago wanted to sell his board game, *The CASHFLOW® Game* but was having trouble.

At age nine, his Rich Dad taught him how to be a rich man by playing *Monopoly.* In 1994, Robert and his wife, Kim, decided to take what they had learned from his dad and create a game board so others could have fun learning.

There are two tracks on his board game, CASHFLOW®:

1. **The Rat Race**
2. **The Fast Track**

The object of the game is to increase your financial IQ to exit the rat race and have more passive income, so you don't have to work anymore, and your money is working for you.

According to the Self-Publishing Hall of Fame, here's the story behind what the book's purpose was:

"Robert Kiyosaki originally self-published Rich Dad, Poor Dad, written with Sharon Lechter, in 1997 as a $15.95 *brochure* designed to attract customers to his website where he could sell his $195 Cashflow® board game.

After selling rights to Warner Business Books in 2000 and appearing on Oprah, he sold millions of copies, with the book sitting on the New York Times bestseller list for four years. By New Year's 2005, the book had sold more than 10 million copies and was the #1 business bestseller for 2004 according to USA Today."

Since Robert could not sell his *Cashflow Game,* he decided to **WRITE A BOOK** that would leave a breadcrumb trail to his game, and his plan worked brilliantly.

His book was an *unexpected* massive hit and sold more than 10 million copies, making him famous!

Next up is one of my favorite clients...

* * *

Matthew David Hurtado, 7-Figure Entrepreneur

Two years after launching Matthew's first book, *Allow: The Law of Least Effort to Receive Your Desires*, I caught up with him and did an interview.

Following is an excerpt from that interview.

Matthew, why did you work with me on launching your first book, "Allow"?

It's time invested. *Who has the time?*

You didn't learn this stuff overnight, and you can't teach somebody how to do it overnight.

They're still going to have to put an ample amount of time to get to where you're at.

So, I'd rather just employ you to do what you do best (launching books to the #1 bestsellers list) and I'll just focus on being better at what I do.

What has this book done for you and your business?

The book has transformed my life.

It was the best decision I have made in my professional career. At the time, I needed to establish a new platform that would launch me to where I'm at today.

So, building the theme around that book and then the credibility that you brought to the table with the #1 bestseller status really opens the door for me to make that connection with someone.

Now I'm an authority, and I have the credibility that gets me in the door, so I can deliver.

How have you used the book since the initial launch?

The book is like a very long sales letter. It brings people into my world where I talk about some of the products and services that I offer. Because I share a lot of transformative value upfront with people, they like and trust me, and they get to know me through the book. It's like I'm having a face-to-face conversation with them.

As a result of the connection and conversation, they've already decided they want to work with me. So, I've been able to launch a coaching platform that has been tremendously successful in conjunction with my products business. I've tripled my product business in the last two years.

A lot of this success has to do with the book because the book has gotten me into a lot of doors that I wouldn't have normally been able to enter.

I'm not a doctor. I'm not a celebrity on TV, so how am I going to get that authority status?

Well, that's what the book going to #1 bestseller did for me. It got me authority status, and people now think: "Hey, this guy knows what he is talking about." I deliver so much value; it's a perfect combination.

How was your business before the book?

Before the book, I only sold products. I didn't have my coaching platform. I was doing well. But I decided to get smart and leverage my sales capacity using a proper book.

Dan Kennedy really opened my eyes when he said, "Everybody should have a book because it really is a modern-day business card, and it opens the door to many places you would normally not get into."

As soon as I heard Dan Kennedy say that, I attracted you into my life. And I thought, "This is going to be great." You could do all the heavy lifting for me, and all I had to do was sit back and think about what would happen when the reader got to the end of my book. I strategized exactly what would happen when they opened my book, and I figured out what I wanted them to do. Then, we laid it the book out that way. It's the perfect sales funnel.

What was your free gift offer in your book?

I offered a 10-minute consultation as a free gift at the beginning of the book.

I don't need an hour to get to what's blocking somebody; just 10 minutes.

I learned how the mind works. The first thing somebody says as an answer is an obsession, the second thing is fluff, and the third thing is the heart of the matter.

So, during my 10-minute consultation, I would ask the person where they were stuck in life and five reasons they were stuck there. I would talk about the third reason they would give me.

During this 10-minute consultation, they instantly knew that I knew what I was talking about because I could get to the heart of the matter quickly. Once they had confidence in me, the next logical step was to work with me in my coaching program.

I've sold out on all of my coaching packages because of my book. I had three different packages, ranging from $197 to $2997. The majority of people purchased the $2997 10-hour coaching package. I also sold continuity programs with my products through my coaching clients.

I also had a few people do my high ticket done-for-you sales funnel and mini product business with price points between $25k to $50k and up. I sold three of those packages, and it went really well. That book made me over $100K, and that was before I got serious about it.

Once I got serious about it, I started producing content on YouTube and optimizing the content to build a subscriber list. I always refer to my book as the *free value incentive* for prospects to get on my list. That way, I keep relevant. I have followers on Facebook, YouTube, and my email list, plus they subscribe to all these things on my website.

I'm building that audience size with new people, which is setting things up so I can launch more books and do more things in the future.

How much have you made from your product business because of the book?

That $100k profit is not including what it did for my product business – that's just from coaching. My product business has tripled since the launch of my first book. I was doing close to $15k net when I started, and now I'm doing six figures in the last 30 days. In just product alone, it was over $50k in the last 30 days.

My product business is growing exponentially. In my opinion, you really have to have a book that gives you that authority status.

I selected the topic of the law of attraction because that was trending, and I didn't want to have to reinvent the wheel.

Now, I'm getting ready to launch my next book with you, *Ask Until It is Given*. I'm excited about it!

* * *

Looking at the four case studies above, we see that you can write a book to sell just about anything from vitamins and supplements, to software, to high-ticket coaching, to certifications, to board games, and more.

The next chapter is all about the **12 Profit Paths** you can create around your book to build a lucrative 6-figure business and beyond, just like the author-preneurs you just read about.

Chapter 2

12 Profit Paths to Unlock Your Book's 6-Figure Potential

Here comes the fun part!

In this chapter, you will learn about the different profit paths you can create on the backend of your book.

You saw how Mike Michalowicz, Brendon Burchard, Russell Brunson, and Matthew David Hurtado all built massively successful businesses using their books as lead magnets, income generators, and list-building tools.

Now it's your turn.

Here are 12 profit paths for your book to get started. Also, be sure to check out the **Bonus: 100 Ways to Make $100k** in the back of this book!

Just know there are endless ways to create income streams from your book, whether you are a non-fiction author or a fiction author.

Profit Path #1 – Digital Online Course/ Advanced Training Program Based on the Book

This is my favorite method because it is how I started my online business in 2005. I was teaching a class called *"How to Quit Your Job and Follow Your Dreams"* at Adult Education Centers, Community Colleges, Unity churches, and other local venues. One day, I realized I could reach a lot more people if I created a website and taught my course online.

Within my first 30 days, I made $2,500, and I was hooked on making money online! At the time, I was selling my **Quit Your Job & Follow Your Dreams** 6-week online course, and it was going really well.

It's important to know that you don't want to put *all* of your content in the book you write and publish; leave out some of the advanced material for your online course.

We'll talk more about that in the next chapter, where I discuss the three types of books you should be writing if you want to generate new income streams.

There are several ways to create a digital course and sell it online. Since I've had an online business for 16 years now, I'm going to give you three of the easiest ways:

1. If you have a website and blog with traffic, create a sales page and sell your course from your website. You can deliver it easily by sending PDFs or video links in an autoresponder sequence using email providers like

AWeber or mailchimp. This is the simplest and least technical way to start generating income.

2. If you don't have a website, you can easily create a course on platforms like Thinkific (this is what I use) or Teachable and sell it there.

3. Build a website on WordPress and install a membership plugin like Wishlist and put all of your course material in the training site. Once someone signs up for your course, they will get a username and login and be able to access your course 24/7.

Many authors use the book as a starting point for their online courses and go deeper into the subject matter. Your book is the perfect outline for your online course!

You can't include everything in a book; there just isn't enough time or room. An online course is a great place to provide additional material that would make it very appealing to your prospects.

If desired, have different price points for the online course with various added benefits.

For example, you could add a private Facebook Group, Email Coaching, Group Coaching, or 1:1 Coaching and charge more.

Next up is…

Profit Path #2 – Paid Webinar Training

Sandi Krakowski, 7-Figure Entrepreneur, has made millions with social media, was teaching a 2-hour webinar several years ago for $47. I paid for and attended that webinar. Sandi had 500 spots open for the webinar and used paid advertising, her email list, and social media to drive traffic and register attendees. She sold all 500 spots and made a whopping $23,500.

If you did that four times per year, you would generate close to six figures in income just from eight hours of your time!

Of course, you would have to do some pre-work, like creating the webinar landing page and running paid ads, but the return on investment could be huge.

People love engaging with authors and being able to ask questions directly. Also, the low price point of $47 makes it affordable and accessible.

Profit Path #3 – Membership Site with Additional Content Dripped Monthly

I recently started following Carrie Green, the Founder and CEO of the Female Entrepreneur Association, and ran some numbers on her $37 per month membership site. It turns out she has over 4,500 members, which generates about $166,500 per month in revenue!

That's huge! Six figures per month from a $37 per month membership program! Unbelievable!

Don't think running a program like hers doesn't require a massive amount of work behind the scenes because it absolutely does. She likely has a huge team to support her efforts.

However, I wanted you to see the numbers behind a successful membership site like hers.

If your book and niche topic is something that you can continue to teach and build on, having a membership site makes sense and is also a great way to have *predictable paychecks*!

Profit Path #4 – Live Workshop or Seminar

I recently attended a 4-day event with Coach Christian Michelson in Ft. Lauderdale, Florida, and I watched him make four offers during the event and generate seven figures in income!

Christian is the author of a few different books and gives away tickets to his live events for those in his $199/month membership program. Let me clarify that he charges $99 for the event, but he returns the money to you in cash on Day 3 of the event to ensure people show up to it.

If you are selling a high-end mastermind or year-long program, inviting people to a 3-day event is a great way to get people to raise their hand.

Once prospects are at your event, you want to deliver valuable content, build the relationship, and then offer your high-ticket programs.

He sold $99 tickets to the event, refunded them to attendees on the third day, and then generated $1 million in sales at the event. There were probably 200+ people at the event.

Profit Path #5 – High-Ticket Retreat

I've seen week-long retreats selling for $25,000 to $30,000! People love to take luxury *working vacations* that they can also write off as a business expense.

Gina Devee of **Divine Living** has several different programs, such as her 12-month live course and her 90-day Elite Private Coaching. She also has week-long retreat to luxurious locations.

Carolin Soldo, another 7-figure income earner, offers a package that she calls her *"Powerhouse Coaching,"* and I believe it is the highest level she offers and sells for around $35,000.

People want transformation more than anything. Spending a week with someone who can guide them and hold their hand via coaching is a great way to achieve that.

If you are looking for a high-ticket product to sell on the back end of your book, consider creating a high-ticket week-long retreat that others would love to attend.

Profit Path #6 – 8-12 Week High End Coaching or Consulting

I began my online business in 2005, selling online courses for $197. It wasn't until I created my own high-ticket programs ($10K-$35K+) that I started making six figures.

There are a couple of ways to do this.

You can enroll people in an 8-, 10-, or 12-week program and help them get results (transformation) during that time.

If students want to continue working with you, they can join your year-long coaching program for $1,000, $1,500 or $5,000+ per month or more.

I started my first private coaching program at $1000 per month and offered weekly calls and a private Facebook Group. One client = $12,000 in revenue. Not bad for an hour or two of work per week!

The first time I offered it, I filled it up!

Students will always be willing to pay big money to get big results.

If you don't like coaching, then I would recommend creating and selling an online digital course.

Profit Path #7 – Mastermind Group

A Mastermind Group is usually a 6-month or year-long program with the VIP or Elite group of your best clients.

Shanda Sumpter, founder of HeartCore Business and best-selling author of *Core Calling: How to Build a Business that Gives You a Freedom Lifestyle in 2 Years or Less* currently has a 10-million-dollar business with three main offerings. (She may have others, but these are the ones I know about.

- Pace Club – helping members build an email list and following. This is her foundational and starter program for $1,997. It is an information product with coaching.

- Her next offering is a yearlong mastermind group at $1,000 per month, consisting of two calls per month and a private Facebook group.

- She also has an advanced program called *The 1% Club*, and I'm not sure what the investment for that is. I think you must first be a client in the other programs to get invited to this one.

So, think about a mastermind program you can start based on the teachings in your book.

Profit Path #8- Certification

A Certification program is where you teach someone your methodology so they can train others. It's sort of like a "train the trainer" for what you do.

The *Profit First* certification and the *Pumpkin Plan* certification case studies I presented earlier in this book are great examples.

Mike created his own methodology, which he lays out in detail in his books, and then makes an offer. *"Hey if you want to teach this, then I'll certify you."*

It's a brilliant strategy because there is usually a large investment for someone to get certified.

A lady I know wrote a book on how she overcame fibromyalgia, and for $5,000, she certifies others as a "Fibromyalgia Coach."

She created the certification program because her time was limited, and she couldn't help everyone.

If your time is limited, a certification program is a great profit path for you.

Profit Path #9 - Licensing

Barbara Stanny, author of many bestselling books, including *Prince Charming Isn't Coming, Overcoming Underearning, Secrets of 6-Figure Women,* and *Sacred Success,* had a licensing program she called her "Business in a Box."

I'm not sure if she is still doing this, but in the past, you could license two of her programs (*Prince Charming Isn't Coming* and *Secrets of Successful High Earners*) for a yearly fee of $1,350, and then she would allow you to use all of her materials.

Licensing is a great way to have others deliver your materials and get it out there for you. Obviously, you can't be everywhere all the time, so you could have licensees all over the world!

Profit Path #10 – VIP Day

Adding a VIP day on the back end of your book is a high-ticket path to high profits!

Sandi Krakowski charges $18,995 for her full-day VIP program. Here's the description of what she offers:

$18,995.00 for a full day with Sandi: "The day is held in our beautiful downtown Kansas City office. Full day is 5.5 hours in office (9:30-3:00 with lunch), 1-hour session a week before virtually and 1-hour session a week after, virtually. This is the most intensive way to bring results into your social media marketing quickly. You may bring one guest – an assistant or social media manager."

I'm not saying you have to charge $18K+ for your VIP Day. Start at a price point you are comfortable with or a little beyond your comfort zone if you want to challenge yourself. You can raise your prices as you get more VIP Day clients, testimonials, experience, and confidence.

Some Author-preneurs do a VIP Day virtually and charge anywhere between $997 and $9,997. Some do it face-to-face (like Sandi does) and charge $4,997 to $25,000+. Either way, the nice part is a VIP Day has a high-perceived value.

As marketing expert and bestselling author of *The Highly-Paid Expert*, Debbie Allen says:

*"Build value around offering more of your personal time. For example, you can include a pre-program questionnaire and a preview call to help your client get ready for their VIP day. Your program may also include a 30- to 60-day email follow-up before and/or after your VIP day, in order to clarify key points. This guarantees success for both the client and the expert. When you have an expert program that offers solutions, people will begin paying for your time right away. When you can take someone **farther and faster** to see immediate results, they will pay even more for your valuable time."*

VIP Days are a good option if you want to get a fast influx of cash in your business without a long-term coaching commitment.

Profit Path #11 – Done-For-You Service

Jennifer Spivak, also known as the *Facebook Ads girl*, has a Done-For-You Facebook ad service that she sells for $5000 a month with a 4-month minimum (at the time of the writing of this book) and includes the following:

"I'll create your campaigns, design your ads, set your targeting, and even place your pixels so you can breathe easy."

What can you sell as a Done-For-You service on the back end of your book?

Let's say your book is about starting a profitable blog. You could offer a Done-For-You "Set Up Your Blog" service for several hundred dollars and have more add-on features available.

Or, if you are a graphics designer with a book about branding, you could offer Done-For-You logos or branding packages.

Think of a Done-For-You service related to your book that readers would be willing to pay to have done.

If you don't have the skillset to deliver the services, you could partner with someone who does and create a revenue share.

People LOVE Done-For-You services and are willing to pay top dollar for them.

I know because I've done many Done-For-You services over the years, and they are very lucrative.

My previous business coach has someone who handles his Facebook ads (a Done-For-You service provider) for $5,000 per month.

I want to be clear that offering a Done-For-You service is *not passive income*, though. It requires top-notch skills and time. So, if that's not what you're looking for, consider creating a digital online course instead.

Profit Path #12 – Sell A Physical Product

Think about how much movie production companies make on the backend with products such as stuffed animals, tee shirts, mugs, hats, etc.

Is there a physical product that complements your book you could sell that readers would enjoy?

For example, essential oils are very popular right now. If you did a book on the health benefits of essential oils and sold products from your website, you would make money on those tangible products.

You could also create your own monthly "box" subscription service around your book. Let's say you write a book on dog training and then offer a monthly subscription for dog-training products to your readers.

You could also design a custom t-shirt around your book and sell that as well.

The possibilities are endless.

* * *

Fiction authors can also create programs, products, and services to sell on the backend of their books.

For example, my client, Dr. Jeffrey Donner, writes medical mystery and other types of novels. He has been a psychologist for over 30 years and uses a lot of psychological material in his book.

He is currently creating an online course on Emotional Intelligence. He said that the material in his online program would be equivalent to a year or more of therapy with him.

Think about the characters in your book and see if you can come up with a digital course, physical products, or something that goes with the *theme* of your book.

A great example of selling physical products for fiction books is the mega-hit book *50 Shades of Grey*. When I visited their website, I saw they were selling three products:

1. *50 Shades of Grey* Wine.

2. *50 Shades of Grey* Teddy Bear wearing a little black leather outfit and handcuffs.

3. *50 Shades of Grey* sexual toys collection.

Even if you are a fiction writer, you can absolutely sell on the backend of your book.

It looks to me like the *50 Shades of Grey* sales and marketing team (or the author) made affiliate arrangements with these other companies to share in the profits when a sale is made.

Start brainstorming on some ideas of profit paths you can create around your book.

Over the next week, I want you to contemplate this question…

What are at least three favorite ways to add new revenue streams to your book?

Chapter 3

Three Types of Income-Generating Books

Most authors aren't thinking about building a 6-figure business when they write their books (aside from dreaming of BIG royalty checks), so they write books that are *income-blocking* instead of *income-generating.*

In this chapter, I am going to teach you the three types of books to write when using the *Backwards Book Launch* method:

1. The What, but not the How Book

2. The Information Overload Book

3. The Hybrid Book

The What... But Not How Book

Giving the *what* but not the *how* is about teaching others *what* to do, but not *how* to do it.

For example, let's say I am going to write a book on *"How to Create a 6-Figure Automated Webinar Funnel"* to teach people how to drive traffic to their site with Facebook ads and sign-up prospects into high-ticket programs. (I taught this before in my private coaching program, so it's a good example to use.)

Instead of giving readers the detailed step-by-step instructions on how to set it up, I teach them only the "what" by introducing the concepts of funnels and high-ticket programs.

Here's what the steps would look like:

Step 1: Create a 45-minute webinar on your topic.

Step 2: Sign up with Stealth Webinar and have them set up your automated webinar for you.

Step 3: Create a new list in Aweber or another email service provider you use; this list is for your automated webinar attendees.

Step 4: Create follow-up autoresponders to go out daily to the webinar attendees.

Step 5: Create a landing page for people to sign up for your webinar.

Step 6: Provide that landing page link to Stealth so that they can re-create it.

Step 7: Include a link to your Stealth webinar landing page on your website.

Step 8: Set up a thank-you page for visitors who sign up for your automated webinar with a personal video from you.

Step 9: Create your Facebook ad to send people to a landing page to sign up for your webinar.

Step 10: Test various Facebook ads to get your winning ad.

Step 11: Set up scheduling software for prospects to schedule a time to talk to you about the webinar.

Step 12: Conduct strategy sessions to sign up people into your program.

Do you see how these steps are the "what" but not the "how"?

Of course, in this type of book, I would give examples and stories on each step, but I would NOT be teaching the details or the *how* for each step.

You will see this method often used for webinars. The reason experts teach only the *what* and not the *how* is because it's too time-consuming. You can't teach something that takes hours, days, or weeks to learn in a 1-hour webinar or a 100-page book.

The other reason **not** to teach the "what" is because if it is based on technology, then that information could become outdated quickly.

The truth is there is value to teaching people the steps to do something. I paid my coach a lot of money to learn how to set up my automated webinar funnels.

I want you to feel comfortable with this and know that you're not trying to trick people using your book by only giving them the *what* and not the *how*.

Obviously, a book can't teach everything in your brain on the subject (unless you want it to be a 300+ page book, and then people probably won't take the time to read it). People want fast information in easily digestible, bite-sized pieces. They no longer want or expect the manifesto.

It's your job to give them what they want – the information. If they need more clarification, they can sign up for one of your advanced programs to get that additional help.

Many people buy books that have only the "what" and figure out "how" to implement it on their own.

So, remember, in this type of book, you just tell them *what* to do, but not *how* to do it.

Reserve the *how* for your follow-up programs.

The next type of book you could write is…

The Information Overload Book

I remember being on a call with my Coach, Jason, and telling him that I was going to write a book teaching others how to become a #1 bestselling author.

Jason was very confused since I had a high-ticket Done-For-You program. He asked why I wanted to write a book on the topic since it was my "secret sauce" and how I was generating 6-figures in my business.

The answer to his first question about *why* write the book in the first place was that first and foremost, I am a writer, and I love to teach! I also felt it would be a great way to attract new clients into my (Done-For-You) Bestseller program as I would get a lot of exposure with my book.

My coach cautioned me, saying, "*Okay if you have to write this book, then there are only two ways to write it. One is to give the what, but not the how. And the other way is to give them every detail of what you do (making it so overwhelming) that they will be begging to hire you instead of doing it themselves!*"

It's funny he said that because in Case Study #4 above, when I asked my client, Matthew David Hurtado why he hired me, he said:

"*It's time invested. Who has the time?*

You didn't learn this stuff overnight, and you can't teach somebody how to do it overnight.

There's still going to have to put an ample amount of time to get to where you're at.

So, I'd rather just employ you to do what you do, and I'll just focus on being better at what I do."

People who have successful businesses value their time first and foremost. Many don't want you to teach them how to fish; they want to pay you to give them the fish!

That's why I created my Done-For-You programs. I have other less expensive programs available, like my online course based on my book "28 Books to $100K", but my Done-For-You services fill a need in the marketplace for busy entrepreneurs!

I really wanted to teach people exactly what I was doing so they could have the same success. Also, the reality was that I couldn't help everyone. I have very limited spaces in my Done-For-You programs.

So I ended up writing that book, *Bestseller in 30 Days*, and I gave readers everything I knew about getting books to the bestsellers list. My "information overload" strategy worked because many of the book's readers have hired me. They often tell me that they hired me because the information about the process was too overwhelming for them to do it themselves.

Publishing *Bestseller in 30 Days* has helped my business grow in multiple ways, such as new people learning about who I am; new subscribers to my email list; new potential clients for my Bestseller programs; new income generated; and new sales of my books on Amazon.

You might want to consider writing an *information overload* book because you can't help everyone in the world with your programs. For some of my programs, space is limited.

So, this type of book would allow you to share your knowledge with a lot of people while bringing new clients to your door.

Again, think about how many clients you can take into your programs. If you are selling Done-For-You services, how many clients can you realistically work with at the same time? If space is limited, then this is a good type of book to write.

If you can teach an unlimited amount of people, then write the *what but not the how book* instead.

Another reason to write an *information overload book* is because people don't usually realize how much work is actually involved in what you are teaching them.

I know that saying "Become a #1 Bestselling Author" sounds easy, but it's not. It takes a lot of work on the backend for us to create and publish a high-quality book and get that book to #1 on multiple bestsellers lists.

One of my Amazon Bestseller clients, Shellee Howard, came to me with no book title and no idea on what "type" of book to write. She felt her business needed a book to attract new clients, make more money, and elevate her authority so she could become the go-to expert in her industry.

We went back and forth between doing the *what but not the how book* OR the *information overload book*.

Shellee Howard is a college consultant with a business that helps families get their kids into the college of their dreams at the lowest tuition possible. The last time I checked, she charges over $5000 for her services, and her work is very labor-intensive.

After much discussion on which type of book she should do, Shellee decided to give away everything she knows on the subject and write the *information overload book.*

The 3 reasons for this decision were:

1. She can only take on a limited number of clients due to the labor-intensive nature of this type of work.

2. She really wanted to help families send their kids to college.

3. She knew that most people didn't realize all the work involved in getting the result she offers. She felt readers would quickly realize how much work and time is involved, and then they would hire her. Most people don't have the time, skills, energy, or desire to do it themselves.

I'm happy to say we published Shellee's book, *How to Send Your Student to College Without Losing Your Mind or Your Money,* and it's been on the bestsellers list ever since.

Shellee uses the book at networking events and book signings. It is a powerful lead magnet that constantly attracts new clients into her business.

Our strategy worked! I'm very proud of Shellee because she put her heart and soul into this book, and it's really paying off.

She is now considering starting a certification program.

The last type of book you could write is a hybrid of the above two types of books …

The Hybrid

This type of book would be part *"what but not how"* and part *"information overload."*

Let's go back to the example above where I outlined the 12 steps on *"How to create a 6-Figure Automated Webinar Funnel"* and look at those 12 steps again:

Step 1: Create a 45-minute webinar on your topic.

Step 2: Sign up with Stealth Webinar and have them set up your automated webinar for you.

Step 3: Create a new list in Aweber or another email service provider you use; this list is for your automated webinar attendees.

Step 4: Create follow-up autoresponders to go out daily to the webinar attendees.

Step 5: Create a landing page for people to sign up for your webinar.

Step 6: Provide that landing page link to Stealth so that they can re-create it.

Step 7: Include a link to your Stealth webinar landing page on your website.

Step 8: Set up a thank-you page for visitors who sign up for your automated webinar with a personal video from you.

Step 9: Create your Facebook ad to send people to a landing page to sign up for your webinar.

Step 10: Test various Facebook ads to get your winning ad.

Step 11: Set up scheduling software for prospects to schedule a time to talk to you about the webinar.

Step 12: Conduct strategy sessions to sign up people into your program.

In this hybrid book, you would choose a few steps in the process and give the reader the *what* and the *how* on those steps only (all the details/information overload). So, I could pick the first three steps and give them the *what* and the *how*. For steps 4-12, I give them only the *what*. To get the rest of the *"how"* for steps 4-12, readers would have to sign up for my advanced training or coaching.

This type of book leads naturally to your follow-up programs.

Years ago, I was added to Jeff Walker's email list because he was promoting his *Product Launch Formula* program.

Jeff was using the "Sampler" method; he had four video trainings about his Product Launch Formula.

After the last video training, he made an offer for his *Product Launch Formula* program.

Of course, you could take what you already learned in the video training and try to do it on your own, OR you could sign up, pay the fee, and get the expert's help. This option would save you lots of time, energy, and money trying to figure out all the details on your own.

Jeff Walker only gave the "how" in those four training videos. To get the rest of the information, you would have to sign up for his paid program.

It really is a great method of teaching and works well when writing books to attract your ideal clients.

Income-Generating Books

These three types of books I mentioned above are all income-generating books and should get you thinking about a few profit paths for your book.

Once you know the profit path, that will help you decide which type of books you should write.

In this book you are reading; which method do you think I am using?

- The What But Not The How
- Information Overload
- The Hybrid

In this book, I'm using the *what but not the how method.*

The reason I chose this type of book is because I feel that just outlining the material is very valuable information and some readers can take this information and run with it.

Teaching exactly how to implement each of the 12 profit paths I outlined in this book would be extremely difficult without making the book 300+ pages.

So, I give the reader the "what," and they can implement it on their own. If they need help, then my Bestselling Author program is an option for anyone who wants to work directly with me.

You can apply to speak with me about creating a profit path for your book by visiting **bestsellingauthorprogram.com**, filling out the application, and scheduling a time to speak with me.

It makes more sense to give valuable information (the what) and then providing readers a way to reach out to me if they want my help implementing the information (the how).

When thinking about your book, what type do you think would be good to write based on the profit path(s) you selected for your book? Also, consider *why* this type of book is best to write.

- The What But Not The How
- Information Overload
- The Hybrid

Things to consider are:

How many clients can you take on for your backend programs? If this is a small number, consider writing the *information overload book*. If you can take on unlimited clients, I would do the *what but not the how book* or *the hybrid*.

Income-blocking books are long books that teach the *what* and the *how* leaving little opportunity for follow-up programs.

If you taught the *what* and the *how*, then your book would probably be 300 pages or more.

These three types of income-generating books outlined here are designed to lead your readers on a path to working with you on a deeper level and implement your teachings.

It's different for fiction authors because they are writing novels, but they can still sell products on the backend of their book if they think creatively. I shared the *50 Shades of Grey* and Dr. Jeffrey Donner's *Emotional Intelligence* examples in the last chapter.

Fiction authors can make money with products, speaking engagements, and other profit paths by creatively using their books to build a business.

Now it's time to use the 6-figure calculator and chart to see exactly how you can create six figures or more with your book.

Chapter 4

Profit Path Calculator

SHOW ME THE MONEY!

Pick one or two Profit Paths from the list below, set a price point, and create your new 6-figure Income Profit Path for your book:

- Digital Online Course/Training Program Based on the Book (You Can Charge Anywhere From $97 to $1997+ for Your Online Program)

- Paid Webinar Training (I Would Keep This Low-Ticket at $47 or $57)

- Membership Site with Additional Content Dripped Monthly ($27 or $37 a month to make this affordable)

- Live Workshop or Seminar (Charge anywhere from $99 to $2000 per ticket. If you are planning to upsell attendees at the event to your higher-priced program, offer this at a low cost).

- High Ticket Retreat (transformation is the name of the game here; what transformation can you offer at this event? How much is that worth to people? $5k? $10k? $25k? $35k or higher?)

- 8- to 12-Week High-End Coaching or Consulting ($3,000 to $10,000+ is a good price point)

- Mastermind Group ($1K to $5K+ per month)

- Certification ($5K to $10K+)

- Licensing ($1K - $3K+ Per Year)

- VIP Day ($997 to $25K+)

- Done-For-You Service ($5K to $25K+)

- Sell a Physical Product (prices vary)

Fill in the blanks below:

To make six figures from my book, my first path to profit is: _____. I will price that program at $_____ and I will sell _____ number of programs to generate six figures.

Example:

To make six figures from my book, my path to profit will be a digital online course priced at $997 and I will sell 101 of these courses to generate six figures with my book. 101 x $997 = $100,697!

You can add more than one profit path to your book.

You could offer a standalone digital product and upsell those buyers to a 12-week group coaching program for $5000.

Mix and match the profit paths and watch your income soar!

Below is a sample chart showing what creating multiple streams of income with your book can look like.

Program Type	Program Price	Number of Sales	Annual Income Generated
Digital Online Course	$297	350/year 29/month	$103,950
Paid Webinar	$57	500/quarter 2000/year	$116,000
Membership Site	$47/mo.	1000	$564,000
Live Event	$997	150	$149,550
Luxury Retreat	$25K	100	$250,000
8-12 Week Coaching Program	$5000	40/year	$200,000
Private Mastermind	$1000/mo.	120/year 10/month	$120,000
Certification	$5000	24/year 2/month	$120,000
Licensing	$1500	100/year	$150,000
VIP Day	$5000	200/year	$100,000
Done-For-You Service	$3000	48/year 4/month	$144,000
Physical Product	$100	1000	$100,000

Now, it's your turn to create your 6-7 figure Profit Path around your book.

Program Type	Program Price	Number of Sales	Annual Income Generated
Digital Online Course	$		$
Paid Webinar	$		$
Membership Site	$		$
Live Event	$		$
Luxury Retreat	$		$
8-12 Week Coaching Program	$		$
Private Mastermind	$		$
Certification	$		$
Licensing	$		$
VIP Day	$		$
Done-For-You Service	$		$
Physical Product	$		$

Wasn't that fun?

Starting with a digital product is the fastest and easiest way to start generating income around your book.

Once you create a digital course, then it's easier to add on other income streams.

For example, create a 6 to 8-week online course around your book or even a 4-week mini-course.

Don't try to give people everything in the course; just try to help them get a result.

Once your online course is up and running, add an 8-week group coaching program and charge $5000+ to join. The beauty of doing it in this order is that creating the online course forces you to create the content. Adding the high-ticket coaching is easy because you now have the curriculum for the students already set up, allowing you to add weekly group coaching calls.

Brilliant, right?

It's the perfect way to get started.

Then, you can stack these profit paths on top of each other and build a real empire!

Chapter 5

Why Writing Shorter Books are Better & They Have a Higher ROI

Because we live in a high-technology, fast-paced world, we are all very distracted, and our time is fragmented. Gone are the days when people would purchase a 300+ page book on a topic and block out leisurely reading time.

Now our time is broken up into very short and disjointed periods with continual interruptions such as email, text messages, Facebook, Twitter, LinkedIn and Instagram feeds, etc.

Consequently, people have diminished attention spans. They still want to learn new things; they just want to learn them quicker and faster.

Studies have shown that people want shorter books that they can consume in a few hours instead of longer books that they will most likely never finish.

For example, instead of writing a book on the A-Z of Marketing, it's better to write a series of books that focus on one topic. The series could include books on topics such as Writing Persuasive Sales Copy, Creating Facebook Ads, Building a Profitable Blog, How to Create an Automated Webinar, etc.).

So, think about your topic and then break it down into a series of books instead of only one book.

THINK MICRO INSTEAD OF MACRO TOPICS

There's a saying *"Niche and Grow Rich."*

How Keywords Can Help You Figure Out Your Audience and What Book to Write

Amazon is a crowded marketplace where readers find books using *keywords*. Readers enter the keywords that help them find the perfect book to solve their problem.

For example, the book that you are currently reading, ***Backwards Book Launch: Reverse Engineer Your Book to Unlock its Hidden 6-Figure Potential,*** is found with the following seven keywords that I researched and selected when publishing this book:

- ✓ Book Launch

- ✓ 6-Figure Author

- ✓ How to Market a Book

- ✓ Multiple Streams of Income

- ✓ Self-Publishing Books

- ✓ How to Make Money Writing

- ✓ How to Make a Living as a Writer

Figuring out your keywords (especially if you have not written your book yet) will help you get clarity on your topic. Then, you can research how people are searching for information on that particular topic on Amazon.

I often see my clients *guess* which keywords are best for their book, and 99% of the time, they have the *wrong* keywords.

The best way to find the right keywords is by doing a brain dump of what you think readers would enter in a search box to find books about your topic.

If they are, in fact, keywords that buyers are searching for, they will self-populate in the search bar on Amazon. If they don't pop up, you shouldn't use those keywords.

Another tip when you are selecting keywords is to use the title of a competitor's bestselling book for one or two keywords.

My last keyword listed above is *"How to Make a Living as a Writer,"* which is a book written by Joanna Penn that is currently on the bestsellers list. Now, my book will show up in the search results when people enter that keyword phrase.

Once you know your keywords, that will give you more insight and focus into who your ideal audience and reader is.

Keywords can also provide you with some ideas for what books to write. You could actually find keywords from Amazon's search bar and use that as the title of your book.

I use **Publisher Rocket** to do all of my keyword research.

Once you've done some research on the keyword search terms, you can get busy writing a short book on that topic.

10 Reasons Why Writing Shorter Books Is a Great Idea:

1. Time and attention are in short supply.

2. Writing short books is a lot easier than writing long books.

3. You can write short books quickly (it took me three days to write the bulk of this book.) I have tweaked and edited it, but I wrote most of it over a holiday weekend.

4. Volume Boosts Your Visibility (especially on Amazon), and you can attract repeat readers who start to follow you.

5. Short books involve less risk.

6. Short books allow you to create a series of books that explore your favorite subjects in far greater depth than you could do in a single, longer book.

7. The data shows that most people don't get through the first couple of chapters of a book. With short books, there's a better chance people will read your book because they won't feel so overwhelmed by the number of pages in the book.

8. Amazon has a "Short Reads" category. Although you can't select this category when publishing on KDP, if your book meets the page number criteria, Amazon will place your book in that category, and your book will get more exposure.

9. You can price your eBook cheaper to get a higher number of sales. At low price points, people are more willing to purchase while searching. The low cost makes it a "no-brainer" decision.

10. You can niche and grow rich by writing short books that are in very narrow categories and do very well.

Return On Investment (ROI)

I have a book that is over 200 pages and took me two years to write that doesn't sell very well.

In 2020, I wrote a book a month for an entire year, and those short books outsell the longer book 10 to 1. You can read all the details in my book, *28 Books to $100K*.

You are more likely to write and finish a shorter book than a large book because writing large books (50,000 to 75,000-words) can be an overwhelming and daunting task.

When I decided to write a series of *shorter books* between 12,000 and 20,000 words, it was easier, faster, and I was more excited about the project.

Once I was clear on the title, subtitle, and chapters for this book (as well as my profit paths on the backend), I set aside the time to get the book done.

I dedicated four hours a day on Labor Day weekend to write this book. I got 80% of it written in three days by blocking out a large block of time to write!

TYPING IS A GREAT SKILL TO HAVE

For 17 years, I was a paralegal and a legal secretary (my first career), so I type pretty fast (close to 100 words per minute.) I can get a lot done on a book in a short period of time.

If you aren't a fast typist, there are alternatives. You can speak your book into an app on your phone like "Rev" and have it transcribed for $1 per minute of audio recording. Then, edit and clean up the transcript, and voila! You have a book!

After I finished writing the book, I had the cover made by a designer, and then I published it on Amazon Kindle Direct Publishing (KDP). Once the book was published and had at least five reviews, I did a 2-day book launch to #1 bestseller, which I'll talk about later.

Choosing to write short books allowed me to write a book a month for an entire year and create $3,300+ per month in passive income!

I know this might sound crazy to you, and I'm not suggesting you need to do the same thing. I LOVE to write, and I

LOVE to teach, and this is FUN for me! (I recognize that writing books is not "fun" for everyone, and if it's not fun for you, then you can either speak your book or hire a ghostwriter. My ghostwriting team writes books for several of my clients.)

If you write shorter books and add a profit path to the end of the book like I'm teaching you here, you'll get more books published in less time and make more money.

That sounds like a winning recipe to me!

The **Backwards Book Launch method** is about reverse-engineering your book's profits FIRST, not LAST!

Some good questions to ask yourself for these shorter books are:

- What topic are you an expert on?

- What would you love to teach?

- Have you overcome an obstacle that others may need help with?

- Can you create a series of shorter books with this topic?

- Can you write at least three books for a box set or series?

- What profit path do you want to create to help readers implement what you are teaching?

- If you are a fiction writer, what products or programs match the theme of your book(s) that you can sell on the backend?

- How much do you want to make?

Chapter 6

Seven Questions to Ask Before You Write Your Book

You absolutely must know *who* will buy your book and *why* they will buy your book. Don't try to write a broad-topic book that will appeal to the masses.

The books that are doing well are either niche books or ones that solve a specific problem.

When deciding on the topic of your book and the title, here are seven questions you must answer:

1. **Who is your audience?** Many times, authors write books they wish they could have read when they started _____. For example, I wrote a book on how to start a 6-figure business. I wrote that book to my younger self (the person I was when I started my business over a decade ago and the things I wish I knew.) Think about exactly who would buy your book. Maybe you have a business, and you are writing this book to your ideal client. Try to be as narrow as possible when deciding for whom you are writing the book.

2. **What benefits will readers gain from your book?** Make a list of all the benefits readers will gain from reading your book. Don't be afraid to be bold when writing this list. For example, in this book, *"The Backwards Book Launch: Reverse Engineer Your Book and Unlock It's HIDDEN 6-Figure Potential,"* the title sends the message that authors will learn how to make more money with their books by reverse-engineering the process.

3. **What are the top 3-5 benefits readers will gain by reading your book?** Think about the *pain* your reader is experiencing and why they are looking for your book. People are more inclined to buy their way out of something instead of into something. What is your ideal reader buying their way out of? Being broke? Sick? Single? You must be clear on how your book helps minimize or eliminate pain.

4. **Survey Titles for Your Book** –I recommend coming up with as many titles as you can for your book. At least 5-10 if possible. Then, create a survey using Survey-Monkey and find the top two titles. The survey results may even give you insight into your next book or help you create a subtitle. Often, the results will be close for one or two titles. I did a survey for this book to find the best title, and **Backwards Book Launch** was the winner… but a close second was *"The Lazy Author's Guide to a 6-Figure Income,"* so I'll probably write a follow-up book using that title one day!

5. **Use Benefits In Your Subtitle** – Sometimes, the title doesn't clearly say what the book is about, so make sure the subtitle does! It should tell people exactly what they will learn from your book and why they should read it.

6. **Be Bold and Grab the Reader's Attention with your Title and Subtitle** – Gone are the days where you can be "subtle" when coming up with titles. Don't be boring. Some of the best performing books on the market have outrageous titles! For example: *"The Subtle Art of Not Giving a F*ck"* by Mark Manson; *"Love Yourself Like Your Life Depends On It"* (the title isn't so outrageous, but the cover on the book is a silhouette of a man holding a gun to his head with a red heart on his chest and it definitely grabs people's attention); *"You are a Badass"* by Jen Sincero; *"Unlimited Memory"* by Kevin Horsley (big claim). You get the picture. Don't be subtle, shy, or low-key. It's a crowded world, and you've got to stand out!

7. **Add Keywords To Your Title If Possible** – You don't want to start with the keywords, but if you can get one or two of the top keywords for your niche in the title or subtitle, that will help you get more visibility on Amazon.

Knowing your audience is the key to your success.

When writing this book, I knew that it would appeal to people who have already written and published a book as well as those who want to write a book.

Both audiences can apply the strategies I've outlined to add six figures to their book by adding 1-12 income streams.

Chapter 7

Publishing Your Book the Right Way

Publishing Your Book the Right Way is Step 2 of the **Backwards Book Launch Method**. Once you know your profit path, then you can take this step.

In his book, *Perennial Seller*, author Ryan Holiday examines the works of artists and authors to uncover why their work endures and thrives.

At the end of the day, it boils down to this:

"Crappy products don't survive."

Ryan goes on to say that the better your product is, the better your marketing will be. The worse it is, the more time you will have to spend marketing, and the less effective every minute of that marketing. This is precisely why all the "pre-work" matters so much.

It's best to know and strategize beforehand what you are trying to accomplish with your book.

I work together with my clients to create high-quality books. I always tell my clients, *"I don't decide what books will do well; the market decides."*

Focusing on the "pre-work" that Ryan speaks about, knowing who you're writing the book to and why, is a good start.

The writing has to be good. I've found from doing over 250 book launches that even people with high IQs and many college degrees are not always good writers.

That's why I work with some top-notch ghostwriters to get books written for my clients.

Be honest with yourself. If you're not a writer, then can you hire a ghostwriter.

Once you have done the pre-work and outlined your strategy, listed your reasons for writing the book, and determined the benefits for the reader, then you must publish and launch a *quality* product, including:

- A professional cover

- Valuable content that solves a problem (for nonfiction)

- A professionally formatted and edited manuscript

- Selecting the correct keywords and categories so the right people can find your book

- Writing a great book description that sells your book

- Having as many 5 star reviews as possible before you launch the book (minimum of 5)

Once you have a solid foundation and publish your book the right way on Amazon Kindle Direct Publishing (KDP), then you can do a proper "book launch" to get your book out into the world and on to the bestsellers list.

That is Step 3, which is outlined in the next chapter.

Chapter 8

Launching Your Book as a Bestseller

When Hollywood is getting ready to release a new movie, they start promoting it with movie trailers, ads, commercials, pre-showings, and more.

A book launch is very similar. Start spreading the word before you do a proper "book launch," which I will explain here.

The key to getting on a bestsellers list is having a high number of downloads in a short amount of time.

In my Bestselling Author program, I do a two-day massive book launch for my clients' books and get their books to #1 on the Bestsellers List on Amazon. (I also have programs where I launch books to the Wall Street Journal and USA Today Bestsellers lists).

Before I do this, I spend 10-12 weeks getting the book and all the moving parts ready for the book launch.

When everything is set up and the book is published on Amazon with great reviews, I follow these steps:

- **Hire Several Book Promoters to promote the book on scheduled days of launch. I either do a 2-day free** launch of the eBook or a 1-day paid launch with the eBook priced at $0.99.

- Set up automated posts on social media (Twitter, Facebook, Facebook groups, LinkedIn, and Instagram)

- Send out an email about the promotion to my email list that I've been building for 10+ years.

- Capture screenshots of the book on the bestsellers list.

- Create a marketing collage and start promoting it as a bestseller once we get to the bestsellers list.

- Set up media interviews for my client once we get to the #1 bestsellers list.

- Set up Amazon Ads

I am frequently asked, "How many books do you have to sell to get to a bestsellers list?"

Amazon updates their bestsellers lists a few times a day, so it depends on the competition in the categories you selected on the day of the launch.

To get your book to #1 in a category, you must beat the sales ranking of current the #1 book in that category on launch day. It's a numbers game.

I've done book launches that had between 500-4000 downloads in 1-2 days. And I am happy to say I have 100% success getting my clients' books to hit #1 on multiple Bestseller's List.

Sometimes it takes a few hundred sales to get to the #1 Bestseller's List, or it could require a lot more for a highly competitive bestsellers list.

I can't teach all the details about categories, keywords, launches, and bestsellers list in this book because that is beyond its scope.

The goal of this book is to teach you how to build a 6-figure business on the backend of your book and make money as an author.

In the next chapter, I provide a book launch checklist and describe some of the activities involved in a proper launch.

Chapter 9

Backwards Book Launch Checklist

I like to break down my book launches into three phases: *Pre-Launch, Launch,* and *Post-Launch.*

Use this checklist to ensure you are prepared for a successful book launch.

PRE-LAUNCH

- Research your keywords and be sure to use them, if possible, in your title, subtitle, and book description (keywords are the words or phrases readers people in the search bar on Amazon to find your book and similar books).

- 30 days before your launch, post updates on social media about your upcoming book (warm up the audience); write a blog post if you have a blog.

- Decide on 5-10 titles for your book and do a survey using SurveyMonkey.

- Have 2-3 book covers made and post them on social media, asking people to vote for their favorite.

- Decide on a FREE gift to give away with your book to help build your email list and create a landing page. Or, you can send them to your home page on your website to sign up.

- Upload your book 1-3 weeks before the launch so you can get at least five reviews (the more, the better) before the promotion starts. Don't upload your book too far in advance of your launch because your book will only be included on Amazon's "**Hot New Releases**" list for 30 days after it is published. It is great for your book to be featured on this list.

- Once your book is uploaded and approved, start working on getting five reviews.

- Reach out to influencers (press, bloggers, or podcasters) and ask them to promote your book.

- Send a PDF copy of your book to influencers for reviews.

- Create a Facebook event and let friends and friends of friends know about your book launch.

- Write emails to send out to all of your contacts and email list during launch week.

- If you are doing a video trailer, include your free dates or discounted dates for the launch and post it on YouTube two to four weeks before the launch to promote it.

- Upload your book to Amazon KDP and select two DIFFERENT categories.

- Research additional categories and submit to Amazon via a customer support ticket. Although you can only select two categories when uploading your book, Amazon permits you to include up to 10 categories. Ensure you select relevant categories that are not too competitive, so you can rank high on the bestsellers lists.

- Enter your seven keywords based on your research when publishing on Amazon KDP.

- Decide on launch date(s) and either make the book available for free or price it at $.99.

- Submit your book to the book promotion sites 1-2 weeks before your launch starts.

- If you are doing press releases, submit your press releases or find someone on Fiverr.com to submit your press releases to PR sites.

- Purchase a sponsored Facebook post and show it to friends of friends to get some exposure. Do this over three days.

- Go to Fiverr.com and buy some gigs from providers who will tweet your book to hundreds of thousands of people or post it on Facebook.

LAUNCH

- After the pre-launch period, it's time to capture everything and promote your book even more.

- Check your rankings on Amazon and take screenshots when you hit the Bestsellers Lists.

- You will also be on additional bestseller lists that Amazon doesn't show on your product page, so you have to find your book in all the categories you selected manually. Amazon only shows three bestseller lists on your product page (be sure to check international bestseller lists).

- Create a marketing collage and promote on social media once you are a bestseller!

POST-LAUNCH

- Continue to market your book once you are a #1 Bestselling Author; this is not a one-and-done event.

- Immediately set up Amazon Ads after the launch.

- Add the bestseller logo to your cover and resubmit to Amazon.

- Immediately set up media and podcast interviews once you become a bestselling author.

- Ask for reviews of your book from people who downloaded your book, especially if you did a free launch.

- When you have at least 20 reviews, and your book is on a bestsellers list, do a paid promotion with Bookbub.com. BookBub is the largest book promoter on the Internet! They have over 4 million subscribers and can guarantee sales of your book. One of my client's got over 31,000 downloads of her book based on one BookBub promotion.

- Add links to your bestselling book on the home page of your website (if you have one.)

- Include something about your book in your autoresponder series so that you are constantly marketing your book to your list.

Once you become a bestselling author, you hold that title for life. Ensure your cover reflects that, and include it on your social media sites, website, etc.

My books sell about 800+ copies per month (combined total), and if 5% of those readers sign up for my done-for-you program or my online course, that equals multiple six figures in income.

Getting your book on the bestsellers list and keeping it there is paramount to gaining new clients from your book.

The fact is, if you are not on a bestsellers list, your book is invisible on Amazon.

Chapter 10

100 Ways to Make $100K

I created this list for both authors and coaches, consultants, speakers, healers, or entrepreneurs who wants to create multiple streams of income.

See below…

"100 Ways to Make $100K" should get your mind thinking of new ways to add multiple streams of income for your business:

1. **Digital Online Course (6, 8 or 10 Weeks)**

2. **Mini Online Course (4 Weeks or Less)**

3. **Masterclass**

4. **Live Course (Not Pre-Recorded)**

5. **Joint Venture Online Course Taught with Another Instructor**

6. **Membership Site**

7. **1:1 Coaching**

8. **Group Coaching**

9. **Done-With-You Coaching**

10. **Done-For-You Coaching**

11. **Do It Yourself**

12. **Paid Webinar**

13. **Watch Me Do It Live**

14. **Watch With Me Recorded**

15. **Power Hour**

16. **Live Workshop or Seminar**

17. **High Ticket Retreat**

18. **High Ticket Coaching or Consulting**

19. **Mastermind Group**

20. **VIP Half Day**

21. **VIP Full Day**

22. **VIP In Person (1-Day)**

23. **VIP In Person (2-Day)**

24. **Speaking at Events**

25. **Keynote Speech**

26. **Certification Program**

27. **Licensing Intellectual Property**

28. **Business in a Box**

29. **Done-For-You Service**

30. **Done-With-You Service**

31. **Physical Products**

32. **Monthly Box Service**

33. **Private Label Service**

34. **Software**

35. **Private Label Product**

36. **Livestreaming Event**

37. **Sell Affiliate Products**

38. **Sponsorships**

39. **Crowdfunding**

40. **Sell Technical Services such as Virtual Services, SEO services, website design, etc.**

41. **Selling Ad Space on Your Website**

42. **Sponsored Reviews**

43. **Network Affiliate Marketing**

44. **Sell Related Products to your book**

45. **Online Consulting**

46. **Develop an App.**

47. **Translation Services**

48. **Online Magazine or Newspaper**

49. **Podcasting with Sponsors**

50. **Radio Show with Sponsors**

51. **Sell Music**

52. **Sell Your Own Merchandise You Create**

53. **Paid Tweeting**

54. **Sell Stock Photography**

55. **E-Commerce Site**

56. **Email Coaching**

57. **Pay Per Click**

58. **Pay Per View**

59. **Pay Per Project**

60. **Custom Painting**

61. **Arts and Crafts**

62. **Customized Readings**

63. **Sell Skills on Fiverr**

64. **Tech Support**

65. **YouTube Videos on Your Topic with Ads**

66. **Freelance Writing**

67. **Ghostwriting**

68. **Developing Online Courses for Others (Curriculum)**

69. **Sell a Game That You Create (Like *Rich Dad Poor Dad*)**

70. **CDs**

71. **DVDs**

72. **Home Study Program**

73. **Sell Food Products (yours or others)**

74. **Sell Food Services (yours or others)**

75. **Sell Menu Plans**

76. **Tutor Kids**

77. **Write Slogans**

78. **Write Manuals**

79. **Bookkeeping Services**

80. **Accounting Services**

81. **Provide Customer Service**

82. **Relationship Advice**

83. **Virtual Assistant Services**

84. **Peer-to-Peer Lending**

85. **Compilation Book – Have Multiple People Pay to Write a Chapter in a Book That You Publish**

86. **Editing and Proofreading Services**

87. **Social Media Management Services**

88. **Personal Training Services**

89. **Sell Physical Products on Amazon**

90. **Hold Event and Sell Sponsorships**

91. **Grant Writing Services**

92. **Security Services**

93. **Nutrition Plans**

94. **Virtual In-Home Coaching (Design, Feng Shui, or Organization)**

95. **Live In-Home Design Services, Coaching, or Consulting**

96. **Animal Training or Consulting**

97. **Chef Services**

98. **Travel Agent Services**

99. **Genealogy Services or Consulting**

100. **Create an Agency (Facebook Ad agency, Child Care, Nannies, Virtual Assistants, etc.)**

Final Words

Most people don't have the desire, time, or skill set to do these types of book launches, which is why they hire and work with me.

I use a system that I've been developing since 2013 when I first launched my Bestselling Author program. I'm proud and happy to say that I also have an amazing team that works with me putting together these #1 bestseller Done-For-You book launches.

If it's your dream to be a #1 bestselling author and to make money from your book, visit bestsellingauthorprogram.com to set up a time to speak with me.

I love talking to author-preneurs!

Also, I don't want you to think that you won't make any money from your book royalties.

I have several clients that make $1000-$8000+ per month in royalties from their books, but that takes time.

I have another client whose book had over 1000 sales within three months of launching her book.

You can make money from royalties, but it can take time and usually requires that you publish more than one book.

No one has a crystal ball that tells you if your book will take off or not. All you can do is put out a quality book, do a proper book launch, keep your book on the bestsellers list, and then write more books if you feel inclined.

The best strategy to make money is to write books from which you can build multiple income streams on the backend.

By doing this, you increase your reach and impact with readers. It's a win/win!

I hope you've enjoyed reading this book! I enjoyed writing it for you.

I would greatly appreciate your honest review of this book on Amazon. To write a glowing review, visit

https://www.amazon.com/Michelle-Kulp/e/B006D4EQIY/!

Getting reviews is not so easy, but they help the author immensely!

So, if you could find it in your heart to write a review, I will be eternally grateful!

Here's to ALL of your Dreams Coming True!

About The Author

Michelle Kulp left a 17-year career in the legal field to follow her dreams of writing, teaching, and speaking. She started her first website, www.becomea6figurewoman.com, in 2005 to inspire women to live their passions, follow their dreams, and make 6 figures doing what they love!

Since 2013, Michelle has been helping authors write, publish and launch books to the Amazon, Wall Street Journal, and USA Today bestsellers list. To date, she's helped over 250 authors become #1 bestsellers. Michelle has written and published over 20 bestselling books.

You can connect with Michelle at:
www.bestsellingauthorprogram.com

Social Media

Facebook
Facebook.com/michelle.bachteler.kulp/

Facebook group/page:
Facebook.com/groups/28BooksTo100K

LinkedIn
LinkedIn.com/in/michelle-kulp-732b8615/

Twitter
Twitter.com/6figurewoman

Instagram
Instagram.com/michelle.kulp

www.ingramcontent.com/pod-product-compliance
Lightning Source LLC
Chambersburg PA
CBHW072215170526
45158CB00002BA/612